DIARY OF A BLACK WOMAN IN INFORMATION TECHNOLOGY

Self Empowerment Book for Women in Information Technology

CAMILLIA WHITESIDE

Primix Publishing
11620 Wilshire Blvd
Suite 900, West Wilshire Center, Los Angeles, CA, 90025
www.primixpublishing.com
Phone: 1-800-538-5788

Published by Primix Publishing: 03/27/2024

ISBN: 979-8-89194-094-9(sc)
ISBN: 979-8-89194-149-6(hc)
ISBN: 979-8-89194-095-6(e)

Library of Congress Control Number: 2024901315

PRIMIX
PUBLISHING
THE WRITE CHOICE

CONTENTS

I dedicate this book to the women who are making a difference in the InformationTechnology World. I dedicate this book to all the women in the world who are striving to make a difference in the world of technology. My goal is to help empower women from all backgrounds and countries.

In this book, I'll be sharing real life experiences I've had in the IT industry. Yes, we all face challenges in our careers, and yes, we'll get through them. I hope you're ready to laugh, cry, and connect. When we connect, we grow.

Everything in this book are factual topics that relate what is going on in the workforce being a woman. Just know and trust that you are capable of anything and never give up on your dreams and what you are passionate about. Maybe someone shares your enthusiasm and admiration for all that you've grown to be.

To the reader of this book, who is aware that their voice has not been heard, know that I am speaking on your behalf and I sincerely hope that the Information Technology field will undergo positive changes and shifts to a state of equality for all.

DEDICATION

First of all, I want to thank God for writing my dream and for giving me this chance to be an example for other women, girls, and growing people.

To my mom (Timmie), dad (Chris), sister (Brittany), brother (Chris), and nephews (Terrence & Alexander).

Thank you Kal for your love and support through helping me with this book.

I appreciate you.

Chris Galvez for keeping me and the opportunity to learn from you and taking a chance with helping me gain the skills that I need to make it in Information Technology.

My cousin Christel who has been ready to read this book for some time now. I was not motivated at the moment and just recently got back on it after I saw you are pursuing something new in your career.

Thank you The Ella Project (The Ella Project) for giving me the opportunity to be the voice of other women so that other young women have someone to look up to.

Thank you to each one of you who has supported me and brought this book. It means so much to me to know that you love me.

INTRODUCTION

I am so excited for this book and sharing my experience in my field with you. As I look back on my career, it has been a rollercoaster of highs, lows, and surprises. I started writing this book at the lowest point of my life. You will read and experience it in just a few chapters because I am already a winner. You thought you could stop me, but you can't. Nothing can stop me now, and I'm still going strong. You tried to stop me, but it didn't stop me. It just held me back and made me keep going.

Each chapter introduces a reality that takes place in the workplace. Sometimes we do the right thing at the right time, but we don't have the leadership and mentorship to be the leaders that overcome conflict. We also want it to be positive and encouraging, like a phoenix rising from the ashes.

When you have a dream, you pursue it regardless of the challenges that may come your way. One of my favorite poems by the legendary phenomenal woman, Maya Angelou - "Still I Rise". I remember hearing this beautiful poem when I was a child attending Elisha M. Pease Elementary School. Till this day I have a copy of this poem in a picture frame in my closet to remind myself that I am not the only woman going through these struggles and becoming better with struggle and being confident in my skin.

I would describe my personality as being a kindred spirit at times. I can be a bit reserved at times. I have a fun side of me that comes out when she is comfortable around people. I try to screen people to see what people's energy is like. Do you have good energy or bad energy? I am a person who likes being around people and has a good heart. Sometimes it's okay to leave behind people who do not have the same goals as you do.

I often struggled with finding a sense of belonging because I am a very unique individual. I also like to keep my personal life a secret because everyone doesn't have your best interests at heart. Some people will be there for you to help you do good things and inspire you, and others will be praying for your downfall. I continue to use my good fortune to bring goodness into the world and not evil. I will always remain humble no matter how much wealth I possess. I have nothing to boast about because I am blessed and that is all I have to boast about all the time. As long as God got me then I am gonna be alright.

Don't let anyone get in the way of doing what you love. Stay focused and have a positive outlook on what you love doing.

I went to see Beyonce's concert/movie and, yes, it brought me back to myself. I was so glad that Beyonce spoke out about the struggles that Black women face and how many times we have to repeat ourselves to be heard, or act in a way that isn't professional in order to be heard.

I was so messed up inside that I didn't have the courage to write or to be the "voice of reason". I'm comfortable and comfortable with being me. It's okay for others to accept certain people's behavior and when you tell them how you feel or what's bothering you but nothing's been done to fix it.

I will always be me even if you cannot accept me for me and I do not want to be in your life. I have been in a lot of different jobs in my career and I know that I am good at what I do. People still want to beat you up for being who you are. They don't know how hard you have worked to get where you are today. Being a black woman in a corporation is not an easy thing to deal with.

One thing I will not do is sit by and let someone beat me up for saying what I feel, especially when there is no action on my words.

After listening to Beyonce speak about the challenges she faced as a black woman living in a predominantly white environment, I was motivated again. I will finish my book. I will continue to be the black woman who isn't afraid to tell her story. I will be the black woman in my career who can help other women accept themselves and know that they are boss lady.

I will have finished my book by the end of the year and I am the boss. I am on a path to keep growing and nothing will ruin my spirit or ruin my happiness. God has blessed me with a unique gift and a unique calling. It will be difficult, but I will never stop speaking the truth about the unfairness in my industry.

I want whoever is reading this to know that I am back and there is no way the devil can kill me or steal me or destroy me. Evil will never succeed and God yes you will succeed for all that I have done and all that I have learned and yet I go on.

LETTER TO MYSELF

Did you know that Camillia, you will face so many challenges in your career and keep your dreams alive, knowing that at times the path has not been easy? Learning to share your story will help you to help others see that everything you've done has been for the greater good. Just know that this journey has been worth it, and it will continue to be worth it knowing that you are capable of anything you set your mind to.

You had a dream and it's still coming true.

I hope you're still prepared for the challenges you'll face and how you'll overcome them. Some of these obstacles will take time to overcome, but don't give up!

FROM THE BEGINNING

As humans we all have that need to want to be the best at what we do. Discovering your talents can be a challenge when you do not have a clue what you want to do in your life.

At the young age of 15, I found out what my special talent and gift to the world was. Yes, I was in love with fixing computers, being on the computer, and curious about the World Wide Web. All of this was new to me but I loved it. I started fixing my own computer and upgrading it. Being with my computer was so therapeutic at times when you have such a rough life that you are going through. As a teenager I was dealing with so much and it could range from (trying to be accepted into, not being the prettiest , and dealing with rejection). Yes, being a teenager is hard and it was a stressful time in my life. When you find out you must be from a different planet and not like your peers.

As a teenager, I was so curious about learning how to help others with their technical needs such as computers, printers, etc. I did learn that I could make some extra money on the side beside working at the job I had as a teenager. But little did I know that this is what I wanted to do in my life and pursue this as a career. I had a few other things I wanted to do but did not see myself doing that in my life.

Learning to accept myself has been so hard and knowing that I was blessed with a good talent. Looking at myself as such a young person and knowing what I know now. I wish I could have told my younger self that everything you have gone through at that age would make you stronger for the talent you have before you.

I decided to go to Prairie View A & M University and study this as my major. I chose Computer Engineering Technology, where I learned about how a computer works, and what is inside the interior that I was curious about. I met some of the most interesting classmates and professors. It was different for me because I had never been out of the house for a long time and I was trying to make decisions on my own, and I knew I wasn't ready for it.

I was faced with difficulties because I have never studied programming, theory and the inner workings of a computer. In fact, some of my favorite courses were the lab courses because I actually had the chance to practice some of the things I had read about in a book or listened to boring lectures that were either good or bad depending on my ability to tolerate the length of the course.

What I didn't realize was that I was trying as hard as I could to absorb some of this information with the vast amount of time I was spending trying to find my way in the world of higher education.I didn't know much about a lot of things, only what the professors told me. Sometimes when the university had their career fair, we'd have a former successful student who would come back and talk to students. They were once in our shoes before.Some of them were really nice. And some of them think they're better than you because they're making more money and really don't want to help. It was like I was coming back to boast about my success.

Dr. David Kirkpatrick was one of my professors, and he always stressed the importance of updating your resume and building a relationship with the Career Services at the university to get your career off the ground. One of his notable sayings he would always say in class was "Kicking for one day". I didn't realize that there weren't a lot of mentors in my major, especially when it comes to finding someone to relate with. I tried to be curious all the time because I loved the idea of building a computer, fixing a computer, doing logistics, and so on. When you started trying to decide what you were going to do or even try it out, it was always difficult. I was an A student in high school, but now I'm trying to live this new life with the grades that I need to get this degree.

I started networking with my classmates, my professors, and my non major friends. One day I was wondering if we had any software that I could download to my computer to program while I was at my dorm to get a feel for how to use that tool. I ran into a couple of the admin's who managed the computer labs at the College of Engineering. I was doing some volunteer work to build up my resume by getting free experience/knowledge to do the role of an IT Support Technician role. I later found out after graduation that the pay wasn't great and there weren't many women in the field. I was still passionate about my dreams and goals to pursue a career in Information Technology.

When I decided to pursue this career path, I knew it wouldn't be easy. Now I'm going to share everything I've gone through to get here. I'm still optimistic that I can take this career to the next level. Asked myself, "What are you waiting for?"

WHAT ARE YOU
WAITING FOR?

"Fight for the things that you care about. But do it in a way that will lead others to join you."—Ruth Bader Ginsburg

I keep asking myself, "What are you waiting for?" I know there aren't many women in your industry, but don't let that stop you from reaching your goals. Set the bar for others to aspire to the same level of success in Information Technology.

I went through a time in my career where I struggled to find a place to work that accepted me because it was a new concept to a lot of men in this industry who were not accustomed to having a woman in their workplace. Is it worth it?

I remember when I worked at the Trap House. It was exciting for them to say they had a female in Information Technology now. It sometimes made my day to see them see me doing a role that they were most likely seeing a man do. To know that I am capable of anything I set my mind to and that I can do what the men do and better.

When I started getting my first hands-on experience, I started volunteering at my alma mater's Information Technology department. I had a good relationship with several of the IT admin's in the building at which I took all my classes. I went into one of them and expressed my interests and aspirations. At the time, there weren't many women in my industry pursuing a career in the Information Technology field as I did, so I learned a lot from this individual and was eager to learn more.

Once I graduated from college, my career took a backseat because a lot of guys weren't ready to close the gender gap at the time and were not willing to hire me or give me a chance. I would make it close to the finish line and all I heard was, "I don't think you'd be a good fit for our team." I was learning the hard way that my career wasn't a safe space for me as a woman. To know that it had not been diversified yet with women at all. Some men were open to it. My first job was in a call center doing information technology support to internal clients at a very low salary and they were willing to pay overtime because they were way behind in their caseloads.

During this time, I tried to do things in my life that I didn't feel passionate about but I knew my heart was in Information Technology. I didn't give up. I kept working on it. I used to wonder every day what my life would be like if I gave up on the things I enjoyed doing and didn't pursue my aspirations.

NO ROLE MODELS

When I started my career, I didn't have many role models to look up to and ask about their Information Technology experiences. I knew my background was in Engineering, but I chose to focus on the Information Technology side of my career because it was my passion.Having a mentor or role model is important because it can help you in what you are going to expect or may come across in your passionate area. I had other people to talk to but they were in different roles and may have had similar experiences but not what you are experiencing.

I don't see a lot of women in my area, but when I do see one, I'm glad because I can ask them what they've been through in their careers and what's happening right now. How did you get to this point? What were some of the jobs you've worked at? How was your experience?

As I crossed paths with other women in my area of expertise, many of them have gone through similar experiences as me, and it doesn't matter if they're black or white. As women, we think differently than men, and we have different perspectives on what's happening and how to approach the issues we're facing. Out of a few of them they enjoyed that I was bold and willing to be who I would be even if we were not put on the same levels as our male counterparts.

It's important to remember that it's still a man's world in my area, but they're not ready for women to enter the workforce with them yet. They're used to the Good Ole Boys vibe, and they experience things differently than I do. As a reminder, women aren't paid as much as men, and they're often overlooked when it comes to what we bring to the table as far as skills. I hope we continue to see positive change in this area, as we continue to lift each other up.

In addition, the absence of women representation in leadership roles in Information Technology can create a self-fulfilling prophecy. When there aren't many women in leadership positions, it can make it more difficult for others to see themselves in those positions or find mentors and networks of support. I remember asking a woman at one of the companies I had heard so much about to be a mentor and she was not interested in the opportunity to take on that role to help me become me, I felt so disappointed because I had looked up to her. My manager tried to say you need a woman mentor and tried to suggest her but little did that person know she denied me a long time ago. I used to think it was a privilege for someone to look at you and want to be like you, but that wasn't the case.

Speaking from my personal experiences, I wished I had a mentor that I could talk to about the challenges I was facing in my career. Unfortunately, that didn't happen, so I had to make my own personal choices in many situations that I didn't expect to face in my career. Many of the men in my career had mentors.

If someone walks up to me asking me to be their mentor I would be so honored to be. I can help a person in their career growth and development by being there and giving them guidance on their career path. It's not easy for women, especially black women, to make it to the top of the career ladder.. It's hard out there for women and it especially harder for black women when trying to reach the top of your career ladder.

I had a tutoring part time job while working a full time job. Some of the kids I tutored I also became a mentor to them and have helped to find their passion in life. All of them have made me proud today because they have all pursued a career in STEM. I still do keep up with some of them to see how they are doing. Their parents have always expressed to me how grateful they were to have me as their tutor and the great impact that I had on their child.

WHAT ARE THE
ADVANTAGES OF HAVING
A PROFESSIONAL MENTOR
IN YOUR CAREER?

A mentor can help you develop your skills and focus your efforts by setting objectives and providing constructive feedback. A mentor can provide you with valuable experience and expertise. A mentor can also help set professional standards.

A mentor can help keep track of your career progress. By keeping track, the mentor keeps the mentee focused on their goals and on the path to achieving them. They also ensure that the mentee doesn't lose sight of the goals they've set for themselves. Seeing someone else watching can motivate the mentee because they don't want to disappoint the mentor by not meeting their goals.

Mentors can keep you encouraged and inspired to help you overcome obstacles. Mentors can also recognize and articulate their mentee's strengths to build trust. A strong sense of self-worth makes the mentee more confident and less likely to back down from challenges. Mentors can provide impartial advice or perspectives using their relevant expertise and experience.

If you're reading this book and you're asking me to be your mentor, I'd be more than happy to do that because I know how difficult it can be to not have one and try to figure out a way to navigate this challenging corporate culture. We're not perfect and we're going to make mistakes along the way in our careers. Sometimes those mistakes can send us down a very dark road in our careers. If you could see those red flags before they happen, instead of in the middle of the moment, it would really help.

JUST A GIRL/IT'S A MAN'S WORLD

Dealing with the egotist male ego

As we all know the Information Technology field is a male dominated field. Guess what women are getting the opportunity to pursue roles in this field. A lot of people don't expect to see a woman in Information Technology and be able to do things on their own. It's okay to want to do whatever you see fit in your career, regardless of gender. We all have a purpose.

I remember in my career how the men in my field are treated way better and are taken care of way better than the woman could ever be. I often struggled with the feeling that I didn't belong or didn't feel accepted by the people around me.

No one likes having conflict at work, I know I do not. This industry can be stressful especially for a woman in Information Technology. We have to keep continuing to fight for our rights to be in this industry.

Working in a field that can be referred to as a "Good Ole Boys Club" or "It's a Man's World" industry. Women often face issues with trying to find their place in this industry where men dominate this field. I can relate to the growing pains of this industry from being discriminated against, put down, lied on, cheated on, abused, scorn, ganged up on, up and down.

I have been through so much in my industry that I have had several mental breakdowns because of the industry. It's hard to just be the only woman on your team with a whole lot of men. Not having anyone to relate to who you work with. Sometimes I would do my work and be so overwhelmed at times I would go to the restroom to cry to relieve myself from the hurt and pain I am feeling from my job. Superwoman also has her days when she has to still put that cape on and hold the world down. I still put on my big girl panties at the end of the day to make it through all of this.

Women have been fighting for equal rights for a long time and still continuing to fight the good fight. Stand your ground and let your voices be heard. We have arrived and are not going anywhere. We deserve respect, equal pay opportunities, raises and promotions. This is when I realized that this field is a man's world and people are not used to a woman being included in this area.

I joined a different company than what I was used to this time around. Trust me the shit stanked since day one. I was the only female and black on my team with a whole lot of men. I was excited to be working with another female in Information Technology but that did not happen because she decided to go to another team because she was wearing the same shoes as me but a different color. However, I was able to connect with her professionally and ask her questions about her experience. When I see other women in my position, it makes me even more motivated because we share the same aspirations and want to overcome the obstacles that come with being a woman in a male-dominated industry.

As I begin this unfair journey with being the only one like me and not having anyone who could relate to me in my role. They would go to lunch all together and leave me behind (take extended lunches over 2 hours). Yes there were always cliques with them all. I worked harder than they ever would have in their lives. I was never promoted in my area or given a raise. The guys on my team have gotten multiple pay raises and promotions in the same role. I got plenty of praise from the people who had appreciated me for the work I was doing and how good I was at my job. The term I am referring to is "The Good Ole Boys club".

One thing I learned about this situation is that I wish I would have been a little wiser in the situation and left the company after I saw that I have been here for a year and was not awarded any raise or promotion at. Yes, I learned a lot of new skills at this place but my redundancy and not growing in my career. I have asked the manager and my directors several times in my 1:1s "Why am I still in an entry level role? I was not fresh out of college or did not have any skills at all. But another guy on my team who was hired a month later after me was hired on as a level III". I never understood how he amounted to getting that title. I went on questioning this the whole time and still no answers were given to me. I figured it out because I was not a male and women are not being accepted in this field and not given their flowers. I wish I was a boy or they could switch roles to see how much you have to deal with and how they would feel being underestimated as a woman in Information Technology.

Being a woman in the Information Technology field is not easy. Yes please speak up and let your voice be heard. Never let yourself slip into the background when you know you are worth it. Women have fought in the past to have rights. I am not going to keep fighting and I am going to continue to fight the good fight.

Everybody has a gift on Earth that has been given to us. Getting there can sometimes take a lot of ups and downs. But never give up on what you aspire to be. Keep pushing, think positive about it, and never give up.

As a Black Woman in a male dominated field it is easy to lose your focus. There have been times that I had to cry about my job or felt like quitting. My drive has kept me going because I love what I do. If I would have given up, I would have never been able to pave a way for another woman to be able to set foot in the same role. Yes, I have paved a way at one of the companies that I have worked for. I was the first woman to ever work in my area. I feel proud to represent other women no matter what your color is. We all are going to win in Information Technology.

I remember wanting to quit pursuing my dreams in my field when I had to deal with the misogyny of what I love to do. It's okay for the men to do what they want and still get paid even if it was nothing all day. I have had to work harder to prove that women belong in this area. I have fought the good fight. I remember being asked by one of the directors the following question: "Why do not women want to apply for roles in Information Technology?". I responded with the following with tears running down my eyes: "Women are not treated the same as men are and even if we work hard it still comes with misogyny because we can over perform in this field but not be promoted like the men." I am not married and watched with my own eyes how they gave all the newly married men on my team promotions and raises. I took all that hate that had built up and created a wall at my house to remind myself that "I can do anything".

God has given me this gift and I want to continue to use my gift to do his will. Women, we are winning over hearts everyday and letting the workforce know daily how valuable we are. Life is never easy but you're a winner in the end.

This situation really sent me crying because it really hit me hard to know that working for a corporation was not fair. I remember this happened during the time when the world was going crazy. It was time to get promotions and raises for this quarter and guess what, "I did not get a raise or promotion because my manager who barely even knew me decided to write the worst review on me." Remind you I am a hard working individual and I did work hard. Harder than some of the guys on my time. The person who barely did any work for 6 months and was playing the clock got a promotion and raise that year. Here is what the manager told me on my 1:1 and I was the last person on my team to wait to see what was going on.

The review read " It's hard to work with you and team members have to walk over egg shells to work with you. Your attitude is horrible and the outburst about being frustrated about a customer is out of line." The guys on my team gossip and talk about these really horrible people but I can not. After being told this horrible news. I went to Human Resources regarding this situation and the company did nothing to do the right thing.

The sad part is that these people know I am a hard worker and have always heard good things about me. Reflecting on the mirror that wasn't being reflected on that part of the totem pole. The people in Human Resources all sided with my manager and nobody tried to do the right thing regarding this situation. Unfortunately, everyone in the department wanted to be judgmental about it, and none of the other women in the department even had the courage to speak up about it or even try to defend me. They just looked at me like I was crazy.

After I went home I cried and got my resume together so I can find a light at the end of the tunnel to get away from this toxic workplace. I asked the woman who used to work in that area where I was working and she said she was in that role for 3 years and never got a raise or a promotion. It's no secret that women are discriminated against in terms of pay and treatment at the workplace. You'd think that with all the advances in technology, this would be changing, but unfortunately, it hasn't.

Speaking of promotions and knowing this place is not fair at all for a woman of color. I remember everybody on my team was engaged and getting married. I am not engaged or married at all but to me, myself, and I. During this time of unfairness all the men on my team that were getting married were all promoted. Being a male in society and being able to take care of a family was important to them. I am single and not experiencing this journey of being married and have a two salary income. I was told at the time when this happened that I have not been there long enough but one of the guys that got one was hired a month after I started. This was unfair to me as a woman to witness all of this happen in my face knowing that this is not right. I have never experienced anything like this a day in my life in my career.

Working hard everyday and daily, you have to work harder than they do. This year all of the guys got a raise but I did not. This is how I know this was not right. All the guys on my team have gotten engaged and are getting married. I am not engaged or married to anyone but I got Me, Myself, and I. It was time to get promotions and raises. All the guys on my team who got married got promoted and given a raise. I was not even promoted or given a raise. This let me know that they are saying that the male needs more money to take care of a household. If women aspire to have a career and not romantically linked to a family or taking care of their financial obligations is not important. The promotions were not based on hard work, it was based on making sure the male makes more money to financially take care of his family even if it's a two income home.

I saw from my point of view that this new life of being at a new place and opportunity was not fair. Being an independent woman who pays all her bills and working hard on the side to make my dreams come true was not enough. Even if I was getting married during that time I would have never received the same treatment. It's okay for a guy to get married and get a pat on the back for finding a partner that you want to be with for the rest of your life or have a family with. The role of a male is to provide for his family and be a provider. We live in a new age where women are working in this field and to pursue their dreams and goals to be a woman who wants to move up in the Information Technology field.

Let's start off with a scene in my life from a personal experience that I had made when I was working. Yes, I have been disrespected at work by people. Yes, I have cried tears because of it. I was working at a new company and that day I had to try to be a better person. Holding onto demographics being a woman and black can be hard at times because everybody has this stereotype that black women are on edge and can be very vocal about the way they feel.

On this particular day I was confronted in the worst way in the hallway by a male employee. He had the nerves to come to me and started yelling at me about a case. Of course it was very inappropriate, out in the open, in a public place. As I was standing there feeling the worst of the worst. There was male manager that was sitting in his office right where all of this was going on. Not once did that manager try to come to the scene to stop the irate individual from yelling at me at the top of his lungs. After that embarrassing moment, I went straight to the restroom to cry because I did not deserve to be disrespected in that way.

If I would have been the one to show him how Oak Cliff I could be I probably would have gotten a direct go to Human Resource and lost my job. I just chose to walk away from this scene and be a bigger person. Not once did this user try to apologize for his actions. So I went to go tell my manager about the situation and ask could someone else on the team or could he deal with this individual. I'm not going to help someone who doesn't respect me as a human being when I've never done anything disrespectful to them.

Always try your best in any situation to not act out of your feelings at work especially when you are a woman who has dignity and pride. There were a lot of thoughts going through my head at the moment that I wanted to do in my mind but walking away was the best thing to do. I had learned from this experience that women do not have status in the corporate world and are not equal to men in the Information Technology field. It's a hard knock on life for us. Trust me there are not many women role models to learn from or even have a mentor.

HOW TO START
ACCEPTING WOMEN
INTO THE INFORMATION
TECHNOLOGY FIELD

Here are a few tips for users who aren't used to seeing women in the area. Believe me all the good ol' boy clubs need to end. Be adaptable. Change is part of progress and growth.

As black women in the field, we may not be given the opportunity to speak up and have our point of view taken into account. This affects our capacity to bring about positive and lasting change. Be willing to listen to our vision. By having a willingness to listen and show us how you care about our vision in the workplace can lead to a better workplace.

Establishing an equitable work environment. Black women may feel isolated in all white, male-dominated workplaces, which can impede access to support networks.

Be more open about equal pay for women on your team and don't discriminate based on gender or race. Women are already underpaid now more than ever, and we're always striving to be the best version of ourselves to our families, whether we're a wife, mom, or a little bit of both. Don't underestimate the strength of women and all the roles we perform every day.

PRESSURE

Have you ever felt the need to want to do something but you did not feel comfortable about it? We all have been down this road before. I have learned in my career to not do things that you are not comfortable doing at all. Don't ever forget that you are one of a kind and have the power to refuse if you choose.

I finally landed my first paid job outside of contract work. It was a great feeling to finally have the experience to work on this level. The downside was the peer pressure that came with it. I didn't have a lot of experience or mentors in my field that I knew how to handle this kind of behavior. It can be stressful at times because you want to feel at home in a place. One of the things that I'm not comfortable with is going to a happy hour with a bunch of people drinking alcohol. Like I said before, if you don't want to drink, that's fine too. I've been to happy hours before as an intern, but the peer pressure wasn't there when I was there.

The first happy hour I spent with these people was interesting? I drink, but I didn't feel comfortable enough to want to. I see a lot of people come into the bar, pick a drink, and then go out and converse with people. I see some weird behavior going on with these people, and guess what happens? A story to tell or an historical memory to remind myself of. As a person, I always play it safe, and my limit is 1 drink or no drink. Sometimes these drinks bring out the worst people. Sometimes you might hear some things you didn't want to hear about this.

From this experience, I learned that it's OK to say "no" to something you don't want to do and don't let others push you into something you're not comfortable with.

One of the greatest pressures that I've experienced in my career has been making sure that I'm doing my job to the best of my ability. Above all else, it's the pressure to exceed myself. I'm capable of anything if I put my mind to it.

Understanding your job and where you're working can put a lot of pressure on your body especially if you are stressed. When I started my career, I didn't know what else to do. Teaching new skills to make myself more valuable to my team members became a struggle. Sometimes I'd do self-learning after work.

I remember getting a new team member on my team who was a female. I was super excited about this because I had someone on my team who could relate to the pressures of this role and what came with it. Looking through the mirror at times I could see myself in so many ways and the things I struggled with especially when I did not have any reliable help to help me with some of the tools that were being used. The office politics and the new personalities that I was working with.

DEALING WITH HARASSMENT

Harassment encompasses a broad spectrum of offensive conduct. It is generally defined as conduct which demeans, emasculates, and threatens a person. Harassment is characterized by its lack of social and moral legitimacy.

In the legal sense, harassment involves conduct that appears to be distressing, upsetting, or threatening in nature. Traditional forms arise from discriminatory grounds and have the effect of invalidating a person's rights or depriving a person of the benefit of their rights.

When conduct becomes repetitive, it is called bullying. Continuity or repetition and the element of disturbing, alarming or threatening conduct may differentiate it from an insult.

Sexual harassment is one of those topics that most people don't want to hear about. But, yes, it does happen. And, yes, sexual harassment can leave you feeling like you're working in a toxic workplace. Many companies overlook sexual harassment because employees are used to receiving sexual favors from non-spouses in the office.

I was working on my first internship at a company I was really excited to work for. As usual, I was always the only female on my team. Yes, older men would come up to me on a daily basis and try to shoot their arrows at me. They would invite me to happy hour, lunch, go to a movie, etc. I didn't know at the time it was sexual harassment. Most of the time they would just come up to me and stare at my breasts at my table. Of course, sexual harassment isn't taught in college and I was very young and impressionable.

A woman who worked on the site came to me one day and asked to speak to me face-to-face. I said, "What am I going to do?" She asked me to meet her in her office. She started talking to me about my suit, how exposing some of my clothing was, and the gossip she had heard about the intern. She asked if this was happening in the workplace. I said yes. She offered to take me shopping so I could buy better clothes to hide my breasts. She paid for the shopping. She also removed my desk space from the directory so old dirt men wouldn't bother me anymore.

I was at the time working for a corporation. It was my first time working in a corporate environment. I was working for the first time on a contract job for such a low salary. I would go to work every day and I had a male employee who was constantly harassing me because he was considered above us, but he wasn't anywhere near the manager. I felt so uncomfortable at work because he would flirt with me, try to touch me, let alone speak to me as if I was someone else. I would have to remind him that I wasn't his wife, and one more time he would do something I didn't like or speak to me in any way at all.

At the end of the work day, there was a loud disagreement on the floor. My manager asked me what was going on and how long it had been going on. I told my manager at that time that I wanted to sit somewhere else as I didn't feel comfortable sitting near this person. At the time, I was new to corporate and didn't know what to do. It was the first time I had experienced this at a job.

This company decided to hire a new manager, and then everything started happening again, and the new manager didn't care and defended the male employee and told me it was and said it was job to tell me what to do. I did try to reach out to Human Resources on my lunch break to tell them what was going on, but they didn't even pick up the phone, not once. This was a huge red flag for me, because I felt like this agency didn't really care about me, and then I went online and saw other women had experienced the same issues with this company.

I remember arriving at work feeling this dark aura that something bad was about to happen. The next day, I was fired from the company due to the issues between me and the male employee. The male employee was allowed to remain at the company. I was very angry because they chose to perform a show on a Friday afternoon in front of all the employees I worked with. They could have just given me notice the day before that they didn't want me to come back. I was also going through a lot at the time and was crying on the way home.

Have you ever had that day where you just did not care about your appearance when you went to work because you were not trying to draw attention to yourself. Here is a story about dealing with harassment about how you look.

I normally keep my look simple and basic when I go to work. This time I decided to go get my hair done in the middle of the week since I had things to do that weekend. I remember going to work the day before with my hair in a ponytail but the next day I got my hair done and decided to put on makeup since my hair was curled up really nice. I went to work and got so many compliments from all types of people that day.

One of the most disrespectful comments I got was from my manager. He asked me to come into his office to talk. I went into the office to talk and he harassed me. So my manager gave me all of these nice compliments and then had the nerves to tell me he did not mind me going to get my hair done during the week. He also offered to pay for it as well. Being a woman who has standards and self respect I declined the offer because it was downright disrespectful to me. My manager is married and has a wife who barely speaks English. Yes, she comes to the office on a regular basis. My conscience would have not set well with that type of offer from my manager who is a married man and I am not about to be a rumor about office drama.

Harassment (bullying) is another form of harassment. Bullying or psychological abuse is unacceptable in the workplace, but it does happen. I was bullied before at a job, and it didn't help me become more positive in my life because it left me feeling like I was in a bad place. I was really excited to work for this company, but it wasn't what I thought it would be.

Let's start with this. I was in this position for a very short period of time. Every day was a battle with the manager. He thought I was lying or didn't know how to do my job. In a new company, it takes 6 months to learn the job and role. Every day the manager was looking for a way to demean me. I wasn't the only one who was demeaned. This person bullied employees, team members and vendors.

He abused his position as a leader within the company. He was unstoppable within the upper leadership team. He was given multiple opportunities to improve but no action was taken. The bullying began more when a new team member joined the team. The new team member was thought of much higher than me and was automatically made a senior. This was unfair to me. I was constantly being cold-shone and accused of lying about my skills. I never had the chance to show my skills because I kept getting kicked. Nothing positive came out of their mouths. It got to the point that I was depressed about working every day. I was dead inside because my passion for Information Technology had become my death. I began to feel isolated in my role. Access was being taken away.

All the red flags that occurred while I was in this position helped me to understand that sometimes things don't look good on the outside. It ended and I was so relieved to be rid of the negativity, the unnecessary drama, the feeling like I didn't belong. I was speaking up for myself a lot in this role, and this person didn't like me speaking up for myself and being well informed about my approach to Technology. I think the bullying came from a sense of jealousy that I as a person could take on the leadership role he was in and do better than what was happening.

Being bullied in the workplace was one of the worst experiences I've ever had and it's made me a better person. I've learned that I don't deserve to be treated this way as a person and that I deserve respect.

No one should ever feel like they're being bullied in the workplace. If that's the case for you, then this is a sign that you're ready to move away from that toxic workplace environment. You're worth more than being taken advantage of because you don't want to feel small. Your mental well-being is more important to you than dealing with the trauma that can leave you feeling depressed or at a dark point in your life. Don't be afraid to stand up for yourself. You deserve better in your career and you deserve to feel good about yourself. Everyone wants to feel good about themselves and that they're making a positive impact in their life to do their passion that they love.

LISTEN

Never let your voice not be
heard in the workplace

Yes, I've been ignored by men in my career. Believe me, it's no fun being ignored when you've got a great idea or want to talk about something.I remember being at a meeting at work once and all the guys were talking.I had to come in as a bit sassy to get them to listen to me or shout a little louder. Here are a few times I felt like my voice wasn't being heard.

Don't ever forget that you have the power to speak up and don't let anyone shut you up or make you feel like you aren't as powerful as you are. It's amazing to be that amazing woman with character. In my Maya Angelou voice "Does my sassiness upset you?"Still I Rise by Maya Angelou.

If people won't let you talk honestly and don't act like they didn't hear you or what you have to say. Speak up and here are some things to to think about next time you are in a meeting but feel like you aren't heard.

I remember sitting at a meeting at work, listening to all the guys discussing their ideas. Believe me your girl is sitting in the back listening to ideas or what I have said in past meetings before.

Once I realized that my voice wasn't being heard I started writing down all the dates I talked about that idea to let them know that I wasn't dumb. When they brought up an idea that they thought was cool I gave them check receipts actions. I would sneer and say, "I brought up that idea at this meeting." Do to the fact that they didn't want to hear me or they made it look like I was whining or complaining about what I said. In my Nene Leakes voice, "I said what I said."

From this experience I saw how the others would use my ideas to try to make themselves look good in front of leadership. In my mind the leadership was only concerned about the men's thoughts and not really mine. I am a real person who has feelings and refuses to sit around to be silenced.

Most of the time, people see me as invisible because of my skin color and don't want to listen to me because they don't have the maturity to listen to your perspective or ideas.

I've seen this so many times in my career, and it's been very frustrating in terms of wanting to be listened to.

I remember one time at work, I was asked for my opinion on a subject, and this person was so in their own little world at the time. They would never take anything I said into account, but they would do what they wanted anyway. This created a toxic workplace environment.

This was a huge red flag because I'm human, and I've been through so much in my career.

IT'S OKAY TO CRY

*Talking about overcoming
depression and anxiety*

Yes, I have been through a period of depression in my life where I felt that I was unworthy. I had to find a way to allow my mind to not have negative thoughts and energy surrounding me.

I am human and I have walked around feeling insecure about myself and career. One thing that I have to admit is that I lacked confidence. I don't feel confident because I didn't know where I was going or what my professional career was going to be.

One thing a lot of people do not talk about is depression. Depression does exist and it is real. People deal with this everyday and do not have much support to lean on if others do not understand what you are going through and can not relate with your feelings or thoughts.

Yes, I have been through depression and it has been an easy road to deal with. I remember when I was in high school, I got made fun of because I had Eczema at that moment and not much was known about this growing up. I also dealt with not being the prettiest girl in the whole. I got tired of dealing with the pressure of what I was dealing with and wanted to end my life because I never thought I was worthy of living.

As I got older I started to begin to drink very heavily when I was in college to get rid of all the pain that I was going through as a person. I was going through family issues, stress of school, toxic relationships, and trying to fit in. I was so gone in my mind that I was hoping one day not to wake up.

One day I was talking to a mutual friend that cared about me and suggested I go talk to a counselor. I decided to go talk to a counselor and started to heal. Never be afraid to go to counseling. Just know each one of us has a purpose in life. If you ever have those types of feelings, never be scared to tell someone who cares. If you do not feel that person exists be sure to contact a counselor or a program that can help you.

When I started my career, I was struggling with depression and anxiety because I didn't know where to go or what I was going to do. Some of the jobs I've had before have left me feeling depressed because of all the unnecessary stress they put me through and the toll they took on my soul. At times, I felt like the job and the role was a drain on my energy.

Yes the pressure that I faced in my career and not really having too many places to vent or to go regarding my career. I really did not have many roles to lean on or or get advice about what I was going through. I am always talking about taking care of yourself. At the end of the day a lot of these jobs only care about the money being made and not you as a person. They will overwork you to the point where you have been extremely stressed out and crying on the side.

I've worked at a couple of places in my career that have been extremely stressful. In both cases, I never had a work-life balance and was more at work than I was enjoying it. In some cases, the work was so unstructured that I didn't want to work at all.

I don't like being on call. It's never fair. One company I worked for, I lived on the opposite side of town, and I had to drive to work every day because of system outages or system changes that happened in the middle of the night. At the time, I needed money because I was recovering from being out of work. Working in this job made me depressed because of the amount of work I had to do and the never ending nature of it. It made me depressed because the team I worked with made sure they would extend the work so they could get overtime. The team lost members, and it became my only responsibility. I tried to take a vacation or take a sick day but I couldn't because I didn't have a reliable person to help me and it was difficult to plan because I didn't know what would happen next. People didn't know how to effectively communicate with projects.

I am not really a fan of being on call because it's never a fair situation at all. One of the companies I worked for I lived on a totally different side of town and would have to drive up there because of a system outage or a system change that happened at night. I knew I needed money at the time because I was just recovering from being unemployed. Working this job stressed me out and it made me feel depressed because of all the work that needed to be done and it was never ending. It weighed me down because the team that I was working with made sure that they would prolong the work so that they could get all of this overtime. Then the team lost members and it started to be a sole responsibility in my life. I wanted to take a vacation but could not because there was no reliable person to assist and it was hard to plan because you did not know what obstacle was coming out the woods. People did not know how to communicate effectively with projects. I would go home crying in the middle of the night because I was so exhausted from work and I was so sad because I wanted someone to save me from this life so I could have a better one.

I followed my heart and found a job that was a bit better than where I had been working and paid more, but it came with a lot of stress in a different setting. I moved to a new city where I didn't know anyone, and I was depressed because I was looking for a place where I felt like I belonged. It was difficult to fit in because I knew it was a different kind of work. The people were demanding and sometimes rude. Learning all the new material was difficult in this environment. Little did I know I was going to find out that place was going to really make me feel dead inside by all the unfair things I would see and go through here.

During the pandemic, I found myself in a state of deep depression because I had a lot going on at the time. I was struggling to connect with my loved ones because I was alone at home trying to make sense of my life. I didn't have a husband or a child. It was just me, me, and me.

The work became very difficult as I was the only one going into the office during this period while my team members were working around the clock and trying their best to cram as much work as possible into my schedule.

I had a manager who did not appreciate all the hard work that I was putting in. He gave me a review which was completely untrue to all the work that I was doing. He would give raises and promotions to people who haven't done any work for 6 months.

I was at a loss that day. I had driven home that day crying because it was so painful to think that after all the hard work I had put in, I wouldn't even get a promotion or a raise. Instead, I decided to spend more time at home and update my resume to see if there was a glimmer of hope.

I did find a job, but the manager was very jealous of me and would do his best to psychologically abuse me because he thought we were above the law. This added to the stress of my life as everything had to go his way and was not open to any ideas. He would not give me the opportunity to prove myself as soon as I started working for him. I was paid better but not given better treatment. He would tell me I had lied and that I could do certain things. It takes about 6 months for me to learn my job.I was not satisfied and started to feel like my career choice was not the best to be in.

Throughout my career, I had to deal with the intense stress of depression. Every day, I tried not to let it get the best of me. I focused on all of that and turned it into fire to keep going. Many people didn't know that I was walking around smiling, but little did they know I had all of that hurt in my heart. I am fine and I have learned to cope with it by being positive and saying positive affirmations in my head every day.

TAKE CARE OF YOURSELF

Taking care of your Mental Health is important. It is to take care of yourself.

I often say to myself, "I need to look out for myself more than I do the people and business I work for," but the truth is, a lot of companies don't care if you're mentally stressed. They don't check on the people who work in information technology because all you're thinking about is that the issue you have is worth screaming/stressing those people who put their lives on the line to keep the company going.

As a career woman I have been through stressing situations at my work place where I did not have a work life balance to rest and reflect. It's easy to get burned out at a job when you are good at what you do and no one wants to help these users.

I may look strong on the outside but I am emotional on the inside. Dealing with work stress has caused me to cry, become an alcoholic, and feel unworthy of being a human. The stress of working in a toxic workplace has also caused me to gain weight.

I remember when I started a new job in a new city and how hard it was to transition to what I was used to working for and with it. I was introduced to the Good Ole Boys club. Women were not respected in this area or promoted. During this time of life I was stressed out with this new place and knowing that it was not fair at all. I was doing all of this work and not being paid my worth at all. There would be times I would go to the bathroom to go cry to relieve my stress. Sometimes it would turn into going into a conference room or the car to do so.

I have experienced stress in a workspace but not like this. I was holding down a whole company that's around the world by myself. The worst feeling I ever felt was working during Covid and being the only one on my team going in. During that time I was not recognized for doing that or even promoted. I was told I did not deserve a promotion or raise by a manager who barely knew me and he gave someone a raise who was barely working for 6 months. It was not fair to me and yes I was heartbroken inside. I was upset and I started to cry and ball my eyes out. Stress, unfairness, and loss of insight of where I was going in my career was on my mind. The thoughts I had in my mind are "Working in Information Technology as a Woman worth it" and "Do I give the fight to future women in my career".

Now that I'm older, I've learned to set limits on what I'm willing to put my mind to. There were times when I let my work grind to a halt. I didn't say anything, didn't think I needed to take a break, and even when I did, I returned to a mountain of work or 99 problems and useless drama. Knowing that your coworkers didn't know how to do their job effectively without you around.

Deep down, you know you've had enough. You know it's okay to take a break during your workday to do something that relaxes your mind and helps you unwind from the pressures of work and home. No one outside of work knows what you go through when you come home. The only people who might know are the people you want to talk to about what's going on in your life right now. Family and friends can be limited in their support, especially when they don't know what you're going through or what to do during your downtime.

Learning new ways to cope with your mental health is a life lesson in itself. I don't have many people I can talk to and vent to. I used to write my feelings down in my journal and sometimes I would just listen to music or go for a drive just to get away from everything going on in my head.

There are resources for positivity to help you through what you are going through. I've gone to counseling to talk to a stranger and cry to let out some tears. I feel good knowing that this person is keeping my life information private. I'm not a private person and I don't feel comfortable sharing all my business on social media for people who could care less about you. They just want to show you how perfect your life is when life isn't perfect. We all experience things in life that are good and bad.

BEING UNEMPLOYED

Some of us will join the ranks of the unemployed at some point in our lives. It can happen to anyone at any point in their career. Just make sure you're ready for it and have enough money saved up to cover your expenses. The tech industry can be difficult, especially with the current economic climate. Stay optimistic and positive during this phase of your life. Just because you got rejected doesn't mean there isn't a job waiting for you. Yes, we've all been there. It's the moment that changes your life. The moment you have the courage to start a new chapter and love the place you're meant to work.

Yes, I've been unemployed before for a long period of time. Believe me, it was the worst time in my life. I didn't understand why I was the only one who had to go through it. It was one of the most difficult experiences of my life. I tried to be patient and wait for them to open the door, but I couldn't because I was running out of money and I was talking about being in the red.

I started searching for new career opportunities and during this time, I was surprised by some of the responses I was receiving during the interview process. Adulting, I know how difficult it can be to find a job. I know how frustrating it can be.

I attended a job interview. I passed all the interview questions with flying colors. I was wearing an immaculate suit. I walked into the interview room with confidence that I had won the job already. At the end of the interview, the manager said that the interview went well but that he didn't think that I was the right person for the job. I was so heartbroken because I was ready to start a new job. I had to start over.

One thing I learned from this experience is that it's okay to be rejected and move on to the next step until that next step opens up for you.

I've heard some of the language from "Not being a good cultural fit".

One of the first things I noticed early on in my career was that because some of these companies are not minority friendly but say they, they don't treat you the same way they treat their peers. Remember, I already have two X's because I'm a woman and I'm black. I know I have to work hard to get noticed, but even when I work hard, I did not get rewarded for it.

If you're applying for a job, always check the website and social media to see what diversity looks like. It'll save you time if you don't even want to apply in the first place. When I check the website, I'm looking for people that look like me. I want to feel like I belong to a company. It's helped me now because I want to see people that aren't all the same color at the top. Working in a corporation is already a challenge because they have different views about what they expect our characters to be like when they have no idea where you come from.

Always work for a company that values your talent and not just uses you as a face for their diversity statistics. It's already difficult working for a company because they have preconceived notions about how they want their characters to look when they don't know who you are.

Here a few tips to help you if you are going through this tough time in life and waiting on your next adventure

- Be positive. It's easy to fall into depression or anxiety when you're out of work.
- Reading a book that you have been wanting to read during this chapter in your life.
- Find some fun things you can do every day to get out of the house so you don't go crazy from checking your email or waiting for someone to call.
- Choose a specific time to take a look at the job board. I chose the late evening and early morning slots.

Know that the right job for you will come up. Don't push yourself too hard or act too hopeless. Sometimes I find that it's because you didn't get that job because there's something better out there. If you're worried about money, try to find a side hustle or part-time job to make some extra cash. Just don't lose hope or lose sight of what you're trying to achieve right now. Finding a job is a job in itself.

POSITIVITY

Self Esteem is the ability to feel good about yourself. Sometimes you need to be your own best friend to help you through the ups and downs of life.

One of the biggest benefits of having the right people on your side is when you're making big changes in your life or career. Negativity can hold you back for a long time. I've seen how my negativity has held me back and how I could have handled myself better when I was trying to stay positive. I didn't know positive energy could bring good things into your life.

When I wake up in the morning the first thing I do is thank God for giving me an opportunity to have another day to be able to do something awesome. I struggle with my alarm in the morning and then turn on the radio application on my phone to get motivated.

Some days are worse than others when you're not feeling your best, especially when it comes to your work and personal life. My work was often the source of my negative energy because I didn't feel appreciated, valued or had too much unnecessary drama with my colleagues. You can imagine the dark clouds looming over my head on any given day. Not having the right people around me to motivate me was also a factor. I had to learn to find inspiration on my own to keep going. My job could definitely be an energy vampire daily because it was always what people wanted and dealing with the frustration could kill my vibe.

For a while, I didn't have the motivation to write my book, but now I finally have the motivation because I don't have all my energy drained by work every day. I've had a few jobs where it's been hard and I haven't had a work-life balance to cope with my emotions or recharge my battery.

One of the ways I found my positivity was through self-evaluation. We all have that feeling like some people in my life were only meant to be there for a short period of time and only for that short period of time. I began to build a circle of people who were there for me and wanted me to succeed. There are always people out there who want to take advantage of you or just wait for you to fail. Being successful can be lonely sometimes, especially when you are focused only on your own happiness and success and not on negative energy.

It wasn't easy on this journey to be positive. There are so many things that stand in your way to hold you back or keep you in that same state of negativity. I was doing the pandemic. I was at the lowest point of my life. I started working on myself. I started praying more. I started having faith in myself even though I didn't believe in myself at the time. I started to watch meditation and affirmation videos. I started to keep a positive outlook on myself. I always wanted to show that I had good morals and good values. I don't want to sell my soul just to get to the top. My hard work, my talent is what will take me there.

It's okay to keep your goals and aspirations to yourself and off of social media. We live in a society where people like to share themselves with an audience in order to make it look like they have it all. I had detoxed my mind to not let social media feel like I didn't have enough in my life, that I wasn't good enough to have many of the things I wanted in my life. I started focusing on my dreams and aspirations and not sharing what was going on with the world and became private with myself. I am sure it is affecting a lot of invaluable people in my life that were just sitting online watching my every move instead of uplifting me when I was at a low point in my life. Sometimes people on social media live a life that seems like they're living it, but deep down they're not. The reason I stopped using social media is because I have aspirations and goals in life and I don't want to spend my days being someone else's "entertainment" or posting all day long about myself and taking selfies to show others that I need attention or what I am doing. I've been able to accomplish so much because I've kept what I'm working on or doing to myself. It's helped build up my self-esteem and character more because I know I'm doing it and do not need that mixed emotion of a crowd in my head.

We are all people and we all need to find a way to remain positive. This was my way of staying positive knowing that it had an impact on me. I have observed how this lifestyle has caused a lot of anxiety and depression in society. Everyone wants to feel accepted and special. I also like to feel special. Doing things for myself makes me happy, even if it's saving money to buy a pair of expensive shoes or taking a solo vacation by myself. Don't be afraid to explore who you really are outside of your social media presence. I did it and I'm glad I did.

INDEPENDENT WOMEN

We are all Boss Chicks and are successful.

I'm used to being self-sufficient and independent. I pursued my dream of becoming an Information Technology professional. One of the things I've always done is to pay my bills and look after myself. I'm also someone who appreciates saving money and not living paycheck-to-paycheck like most people. When I look at myself and how fulfilling it is to look after myself and be self-sufficient, I'm reminded of how empowering it is. Being independent isn't for the weak.

I'll never forget the first time I bought my own car. I didn't need any help or anyone else to do it. It felt so good to be able to say, "I did it!" I'm so proud of what I was able to do to meet my needs and desires.

Sometimes I get compliments from other women saying, "You are so brave to do this for yourself and to be able to pay for the things that you want and need for yourself, with me taking care of you."

We all have our seasons and some of us are on an emotional roller coaster trying to survive. Believe in yourself when no one else will. It took me a long time to get where I wanted to be, and sometimes I had to say, "I can't afford that or this, but we can put it on a wish list or a vision board to see where we can go." I changed the story from

"I can't" to "Yes, I can". It's important to keep these positive words in your head. If you stay in that dark place for too long, it's not fair to you or anyone else who is so important in your life.

Being an independent woman comes with the responsibility of being a grown-up. Some women are more resilient than others. As an independent woman, I had the same aspirations and goals as everyone else. I know I have a lot of work to do, but I will keep striving for success. As I learned from being with other women that we are all going to be at different stages in our life. I know I still have a long way to go but I will continue to work towards my goals. We all need some kind of moral support to help us stay strong even when we are at our lowest. We are all going through different stages in life. As we get older and wiser, we are still achieving all of our goals at our age and don't think that age is a thing.

If you don't have a support system, there is nothing wrong with having faith in yourself and believing that you can be your own best friend. I needed to learn to be my best friend to get through that dark place in my life where I kept putting myself off. If I didn't put myself out there, I wouldn't have the motivation or the energy to finish this book. Every day I tell myself that I am the boss and that I can do what I want. It's lonely on the top of the mountain, but don't let the loneliness stop you from getting to the top and say you made it. Yes, Independent, that's what I am, and I think I need to re-listen to "independent" by Lil Boosie and Lil Phat. Women are capable of anything.

If you have toxic people in your life, it's time to evaluate yourself and get rid of those toxic relationships so you can concentrate on your success.

We all have people in our life who don't want us to succeed, or who pray for our failure.

That's why you need to surround yourself with people like you who have the same goals and dreams as you. They are stuck in a storm that they're bringing you into. Inspire to be better every day. Focus on your good goals and dreams. It's okay not to share them with others. I haven't shared my book with many people yet because I wanted to finish it before sharing it with the world.

RESPECT

Never let anyone put you down.
Keep your head up and keep
your eye on the prize.

N ever let anyone disrespect you in your role or as a person. We are all human and all are going through something on a daily basis. Being disrespected is never a good feeling especially when others put you down. If they have nothing positive or uplifting to say, do not give a person that type of energy.

We all aspire to be treated equally in the workplace, but that's not the reality in some of these places. Especially when you don't feel like you belong or don't have a lot of people who look like you or understand what it's like to be a person of color in your own career. Everyone wants to be black when it comes to coding, but nobody wants to be our color.

Throughout my career, I've seen a lot of men being very open and loud in the office and nothing being done about it because he's a man and that's fine. I've also seen men in my area being very rude and disrespectful to the people we work with, but when I have an attitude towards a person, it's problematic because I'm not comfortable saying no to that person and their expectations aren't on the same level as the man's.

We all have to work together and treat others with respect whether we like it or not. This person has been very disrespectful to many people and vendors but nothing will be done. I speak my mind about a situation and I'm the one who suffers the consequences because I'm being rude and I already have a disadvantage because I'm considered or stamped as the angry black woman by people. I'm not even close to that profile or that level when people think of being black. I consider myself an educated black woman that is smart, beautiful and fearless. I must be the one to deal with the unfairness of working in a toxic corporate culture that is never going to be fair to you.

Sometimes it's hard to wake up because you want some of those struggles and obstacles to just go away. Yes, it was a personal issue I had with some places because to really do my job, I needed to feel like I was doing what I was supposed to do whether I was struggling or not.

Deal with all those ungrateful jerks who want to yell at you because they have 99 problems.

Some days I really didn't feel like myself and would struggle with just trying to get myself together for the morning. Now keep in mind I'm a morning person, and I've told a few people that. I would block off my morning schedule from 8 am to 10 am so I can wake up in my mind and accept this person that is not ready to start the day.

When you're working in Information Technology, you're never sure what your day will look like or what challenges you'll face. Believe me, there are some people out there that I wish would be a little more chill when they talk to you. Sometimes, superwoman is fighting with herself. Sometimes Micheal Jackson's song "Wanna to Be Startling Something" would come to mind when something happened at work.

I remember when I was working. Some of the people you meet in person can cause more drama than just their names. I remember Microsoft had an outage and yes, a lady did not respect me for a technology tool that I don't control. After she said her disrespectful comment with an attitude, I said in a nice tone, "I'm having the same problem. I'm not able to send emails either." Believe me, I wish she would grow up today. She came back to me with an attitude and told me that I wasn't doing anything to help her. I asked her what else could I do? She said, "I can provide you with the number to Microsoft. They also have a website that says all systems are down."

She came to me the next day after everything settled down. She had the nerve to apologize to me for being an idiot. Believe me, I am really sorry for the way she spoke to me during the outage. I said it's alright and I understand your frustration.

EXPERIENCING DISCRIMINATION

"Been down, been up, been broke, broke down, bounced back. Been off, been on, been back, what do you know about that?"

Historically, black workers have been discriminated against in the workforce of the United States, despite the fact that they have played a significant role in the development of the United States and in the development of its economy.

I've been through a lot in my life, and I'm still going strong. Bad things have turned into good things. Black woman stereotypes can be tough in your industry, and you don't realize it's not fair to experience what you're experiencing in your professional life. Racism, discrimination and bias can exist in both subtle and overt forms, making it more difficult for black people to succeed and advance in their professional lives.

I was getting ready to graduate from college at this time. I remember one of my professors telling us to make sure you got experience before graduating from college. That meant getting an internship or volunteering.

Trust me I was trying to do that. This is my first time experiencing discrimination at its finest. We would get all dressed up for career day/ job fair day to go around and talk to recruiters from the companies who came to visit the HBCU (Historically Black College & University) I went to. Me and my classmates would go to also pick up free swag and map out who to talk to. One thing a lot of the companies would do was set the bar so high to get an Internship, G.P.A. (3.5 or higher). I did not have a 3.5 G.P.A. with a background in Engineering. We would go to our sister school that was 30 minutes away to get the opportunity to get a chance for an internship. Nobody was asking them for a G.P.A. at all for an internship opportunity.

Experiencing this made me realize that everyone is not treated equally in the workspace. I would be at my career fair disappointed knowing that these companies were not trying to give minorities a chance to make an impact at their company or give us the chance to experience what corporate was like.

I did not get a job offer before I graduated and I applied for graduate school because I do not want to go back home because I did not like the situation that was going on in my hometown. I did not give up hope on trying to get experience when I got to graduate school. I went to the career fair and met with a few recruiters but this time was different. I got an email from one of the companies saying I was accepted for the internship program. I opened the email up and thought this must be a joke. I got a call from Career Services on campus regarding it. I was super excited to be given a chance finally.

Some of them will tell you they care about diversity but they don't. When I moved to a new place, things changed because I saw a lot of people I identify with that didn't have as much diversity as I used to see around me. That's a new thing for me. It was like, oh this is what it's like to be oppressed in my culture and these people have no idea about my culture but just stereotypes.

I've learned over the years that working for companies that talk a lot about diversity but only use you as a way to advertise to other people that you're at that company to devalue other black people who have worked their way up the career ladder and have the skill set to do that job.

I had an experience unlike any other and because I didn't know what my worth was at the time, I wasn't going to know what that was all about. Because one of the forms of discrimination is my pay and the level at which I was categorized. Come to find out I'm sitting in an entry level job at an entry level pay level. I had that experience. If I knew better how to negotiate proper pay and job level, this wouldn't have happened to me. Women are already underpaid when it comes to your role. Like I said before, this is discrimination and unfairness in its best form when all the guys in my team got married and they were rewarded for taking on the role of being the provider by raises and promotions.

Never forget that you are in charge of your career and should always put yourself first in terms of pay regardless of gender or culture. If the company is unwilling to do what is right, walk away and find another company that is better suited for you. Don't wait for the next red flag to pop up and make you mad. Yes I was mad because I thought that raises and promotions are based on performance. I had it wrong and learned from this experience going forth that I would never devalue myself ever again.

As a black woman, too, we are often labeled as "Angry Black Women" which is not the case. We are all very strong and determined individuals who are willing to do whatever it takes to get where we want to be. We are so much more than that. We are showing our true selves in our work and how we feel. We want our voices to be heard and not be drowned out. We want to succeed in our careers and not have to deal with that kind of association.

This title resonates with me because I've had my fair share of people who don't appreciate me for being a black woman who works hard, who is passionate about her work, and who is learning every day how to be more productive.

This isn't fair to me because I feel like I've already been pigeonholed into a box without anyone getting to know me or who I am.

I do occasionally speak to some of my colleagues and some of them have positive things to say about how being a black woman impacts our work ethic.

We already have to be more vocal than others because it's easy for others to ignore us and silent us a culture because they are stuck on that stereotype of what they think a black woman is. They already see us as negative, and some of us see it as a part of who we are. For example, I remember I had a coworker who was very vocal everyday and she was rather loud but that was her personality and I had to learn how to accept her for being herself and not water down her personality for others. We all know someone in our own culture who has this kind of personality, and they come in all colors and shades.

I recall one of the managers trying to sabotage me by giving me a negative review that didn't reflect my work ethic. He listened to my peers who were my colleagues and what some of them saw in me. He didn't try to understand me for who I am. I felt terrible because I love my job and I do it with passion. He doesn't realize that I have daughters and he wouldn't want his daughters to go through what I went through. I remember I was the last one on my team to be interviewed and I thought I would be rewarded for all the hard work I put in. But no, I wasn't given a raise or promotion. I wasn't given any recognition by the company for risking my life to make sure that we got shipments and equipment was shipped. I felt like this person already saw me as an "Angry Black Woman". Never got to know me as a person or had any passion to see me for who I was. Just listening to gossip and taking part in the "Good Ole Boys Club".

I've always worked in places where there was a lot of diversity, but I've never had that in my life until I started to grow more in my career. I've seen how people view black women and how they don't educate themselves about how this culture operates because they have a negative image in their minds from what they've seen in movies or the music that we create but not having the education. When we have more education, or knowledge, it becomes a danger to men.

Do us all a favor and stop using that term when we all don't fit that category in the office. We deserve to be treated with respect because we're ambitious, goal-oriented, driven and well-informed. We don't come to the office to belittle you. We're here to bring not only diversity into the workplace but our expertise and ideas as well.

Black Women are one of the most educated women knowing a successful one doing great in their career is motivating. A lot of us do not get far in our career because of the reception we have been viewed as. We are not valued as other associates and do not get paid daily because of what we identify as.

I was good at my job and the company knew it, but it didn't show up in the company's eyes to promote me and pay me more. I'm speaking from personal experience because I've been in a couple of different jobs and I've seen other people get promotions and raises and yet

I'm still at the same level of pay and level requirements that I was at when I entered the company. It's a sign of discrimination because we're still not at the same level as everyone else in the office, but I'm an educated woman and I'm showing my value and what I'm capable of. It was a huge red flag early on in my career that I wasn't being treated fairly or evaluated appropriately for my performance, and instead the company was looking for other reasons to hold me back instead of lifting me up.

These people might have thought they could bully me but guess what I'm still climbing to the top of? Just because you did something to me doesn't mean that you can do the same to you. I remember being demoted low key because the manager was so jealous of all the good work I had done so far. They hired someone with the same job title as me and they were doing everything they could to keep me down. It takes about 6 months to learn how to do a job at a company and how it works. Guess what happened after I left the company this person got demoted and they got a new manager over them. You should always be careful how you deal with people because it could come back to haunt you in another form or shape.

I always try to treat others with respect even when they are treating me badly and when I am sick of it, it is time to pray every week about my situation. Believe me God knows everything that is going on in your life.

SETTING BOUNDARIES

*When you talk about boundaries,
you're talking about physical
boundaries, emotional boundaries,
and mental boundaries.*

One of the biggest challenges I faced in my career was setting boundaries. I didn't know what that meant, and when I did try to set boundaries, it usually backfired. I was seen as an aggressive person or someone who didn't want to do their job. I used to be really stressed out at work because of all the issues that I had to deal with every day. At times when I was working, I would just want to be alone so I could concentrate on what I had to do that day. I remember telling my manager that I wasn't a morning person and that sometimes it took me a while to wake up. He would never try to understand my limits in the morning. This person was aware of this and would try to provoke me. This caused a lot of friction in our working relationship and he didn't respect my boundaries. I found it very disrespectful.

When it comes to your work boundaries, be honest and straightforward. Be honest about who you are and what you don't like.

Another thing I learned was to set boundaries in my personal life. I don't like sharing all my innermost thoughts and feelings with people that I work with and don't feel comfortable with. Why should I want you to meet my family when I don't even like you? I don't want my family's photos on my desktop. My family isn't your entertainment. And a lot of people don't respect that, especially in the workplace. I'm like Sade, I like to be mysterious and I still want to be.

When you start to share personal information at work, some people feel like they have a right to be there with you and your loved ones. I was invited to a couple of company functions before and they allow family members to attend. I chose not to attend because I didn't want to meet anyone, my family or anyone else who would ask me sensitive questions about my private life. It's a boundary I set for myself. I want to be the person who doesn't care about me sharing my proudest moments.

Boundaries are an important part of your professional life, and you need to know when and where to set them at work. Here are a few areas to consider when setting boundaries in your professional life:

PHYSICAL BOUNDARIES

Boundaries refer to the physical space you inhabit and the way you interact with others. These boundaries set the tone for how you interact with others and are often about space and touch.

One thing I've learned in dealing with men and women is maintaining appropriate workplace behavior is that in the South, they like to greet you with a hug. I'm not comfortable hugging people. I prefer to shake their hand or shake their hand with a "fist pump" to put an end to the idea that co-workers have sexual feelings towards you in the office. I've been propositioned by both genders before and it can be a mix of emotions. From my experience, I want to maintain my work relationships as work relationships only and nothing more.

Lunch and taking a break is another boundary I feel people don't get. I've had to say "no" to people before because they didn't get that I needed to get something to eat, go for a walk, or go to the bathroom.

When you're working in IT, many people think you're expected to bow down every time they need your help. You're wrong. We're just as human as you are, and we deserve some time for ourselves too. We don't need to be pampered by you just because you want us to. You get to eat and go to the bathroom. Why can't your IT department do the same?

I remember going to lunch after working all morning long. I finally had a chance to take some time for myself. I posted my lunch symbol on the messenger application chat. I wanted people to know that I was setting boundaries and that I was going to take a break. I had a few people that didn't respect my boundaries because they did not agree that I needed personal space for myself to eat lunch. I came back from lunch. Some of these people were mad because I didn't message them back after lunch. They knew that they were being selfish and that I wasn't being respected as a human being. I give you respect when you're in a meeting, you're taking a break or you're having lunch. I deserve the same respect as you.

If you have boundaries, don't let them hold you back. If they don't value you as much as you value them, that's an issue. We're all human, and we have emotions and plans. There is nothing wrong with setting boundaries.

MENTAL BOUNDARIES

Mental boundaries help to regulate your mental energy levels and help you concentrate while you are working.

Avoid overworking yourself by setting limits on when you can work late. If you have a request or need to set a limit, be polite about it.

A working boundary is the setting of your work hours. From my experience, I could have had a better work-life balance. It was challenging at times because people didn't understand that my work hours are set for a purpose. When I was selfish after my work shift, it was a problem.

I remember I wasn't on call that week, but someone called me because the on call person wasn't picking up the phone. This is a red flag that this person wasn't respecting my after work boundaries.

The person got mad and reported me because I had an attitude while helping them. I was already upset because the person who was on call did not help this person and this person called me. I was helping them and the issue was resolved. Me having an attitude did not sit well with this person. I had called into a meeting because "Something was wrong with Camillia, she normally does not act that way towards me". As a person I felt I was in the right because I have the right to set boundaries outside of work.

EMOTIONAL BOUNDARIES

What are emotional boundaries?

Emotional boundaries are an important part of how you manage your emotions in the workplace. They allow you to separate your own emotions from how others may be feeling without invalidating the concept of empathy.

In a workplace, you have no control over the people around you and their experiences. Some people bring what they're going through with them into the office, and it can feel like they're bringing negative energy with them. I've talked about how I didn't want to go to work some days because of stress or it being a toxic work environment. That's a different vibe when people around you are already having a negative morning or day. Most of you probably know that I'm a morning person, and I don't like saying "good morning" to people when I walk into the office. I'm more of a "go to my desk" kind of person. I put my headphones on, I listen to motivational music in the morning, and I do affirmations to help me stay positive. Negative energy from people can rub off on you faster than positive energy.

No matter what was going on in my personal life, I never brought it to the office. I always left it at the door when I came in, and I put a smile on my face to welcome people when I entered the office. My private life can take over after I leave the office. It's already difficult when people don't respect your personal space as a person, and you're working in an environment that can be very unfair because of my color and gender. I tried to put on a brave face every day. I'm already dealing with misogyny, discrimination, and harassment at work.

It's always good to find a way to handle your emotions in a positive way. Especially when people are not treating you with respect. They can talk to each other in a disrespectful way without getting into trouble because they're the majority of the people you work with on a day-to-day basis. I don't have the luxury of acting out too much because I'll be seen as an "Angry Black Woman". We don't get angry, we just build up a wall of negativity until that wall comes crashing down. They don't want to listen to how we're feeling or what's going on. Believe me, you won't break me because this industry has already broken me. I didn't let it get to me.

Don't let people interrupt your show if they aren't having a great day or if they're going through a difficult time.

STEREOTYPES, YES
THIS DOES EXIST?

I'd like to share with you one of my favorite things that I've heard Malcolm X say for years: "The most disrespected person in America is the Black woman. The most unprotected person in America is the Black woman. The most neglected person in America is the Black woman."

This skin color is not invisible at all. Black people work just as hard as any other group in the world. In addition, stereotypes about black people can also create obstacles. We've been robbed of so much, and we're still trying to recover from all the setbacks we've faced in so many areas. This culture is often copied by other cultures, but many people don't understand the challenges we face every day to succeed. But the fight isn't over yet. In the words of Sophia in the movie Color Purple, "I have been fighting all my life."

What I would describe this situation is ignorant behavior. Never assume anything about someone you don't know or are unsure of. I have heard ignorant remarks from women who mistakenly believe that I am a single black mother with children running amok. Instead of drawing that comparison about me, I would appreciate it if you would ask me whether I am a parent. This was something I had never experienced until I moved to a new city and saw firsthand how these people thought, particularly when they are aware that their actions are not right but incorrect.

Little did they know that I was single and educated. Yes I have not made that choice yet to have a child because I want to make sure I am not bringing my child into a toxic environment. I wanted to actually go there with one of them but I did not. I told her in a nice voice " Ask me if I had a child is the correct verbiage to me and not where is your child"? She was not ready for that at all and she felt really uncomfortable making that assumption.

Yes I do want to be a mother one day in life but I have to understand I have to wait my time for that to happen and the right person to come along who I would like to be on that journey with to parent someone. Oftentimes women want to put you in a different box because you do not have a child and want you to feel pressured because of your age. Yes society has changed and more women are choosing a career before having children.

It has been very offensive to me as a person because we all are going to experience life in different paths. I would have negative comments made towards me because I have not had a child yet. It would make me feel uncomfortable being around people because they want to brag about their husbands and children in front of you and not be mindful that there were other unmarried women at the meeting who do not have children. If you and that person had something in common with each other then you can talk about it after meeting with that person.

Many educated Black professionals are entering the corporate world with aspirations, ready to achieve success, but face an inhospitable environment. While corporate America provides a steady paycheck, benefits, and travel opportunities, many Black professionals are missing out on belonging, trust, and respect.

Everybody is different and unique and their own way but when it comes to being a black woman we are always viewed in the same light. It's already that when it comes to us being educated and qualified for an opportunity you are not respected and paid fairly. Some of these companies will use the knowledge that you have to continue to uplift others on your team.

Being one of the smartest cultures you'll ever meet. There are many inventions that people must remember, and this country was founded on the exploitation of black labor and the importation of people from other countries to exploit their dirt and create wealth. They'll be jealous of you because you bring so much knowledge to the table. But they don't know what it's like to be that skin color because they've never gone through what we've gone through. And the more educated you are, the more likely they are to think that you're a target or that you don't deserve to be valued at work.

Black professionals are not only underrepresented in corporate offices but they are also underrepresented and marginalized. As a result, companies risk losing out on significant talent and valuable perspectives that are needed to drive innovation and serve a more diverse customer base.

I remember being the most educated of all my team members. Most of them only had associates degrees or high school diplomas. But none of this meant anything to the company in terms of pay because they didn't want black people to succeed at a certain level.

Here is another example I had when I was enrolled in a summer program. This was probably the first time some of these people had ever seen a black woman. I was shocked, but I decided to take an extra course on my own. I wanted to educate myself more about their culture, and I also wanted to educate them more about some of the stereotypes that my culture has.

Once I realized this, it made me realize how superficial people can be when they've never been exposed to your culture or how they perceive you.

I told them that I can do anything I put my mind to, and I'll do it, and I won't let my culture hold me back. I graduated from a Historically Black College and University (HBCU). I learned a lot from my HBCU experience on "How Black People Created Universities to Continue Their Education." At the time, most universities did not accept black students.I did educate them on what an HBCU was and how it gave other black people the opportunity to become educated. I am thankful that I was able to attend college, and I am thankful for all the people who helped make this possible for us here in the community. Looking back, I know that they faced a lot of obstacles in their careers, but they persevered and became successful role models and created legacies.

After the program was over, I learned so much from these people, and they learned so much from me. They learned that black women are getting college degrees and education, and not all of them are pregnant with different baby daddies and on welfare. I told them that I've been living in a house my whole life and never been on welfare. I also talked to them about black hair and about how we care for our hair and don't have to wash it every day.

Here's another example of how you know how you're being stereotyped. I was in a meeting and I was called by the wrong name. I know that I am a beautiful black and she is also a very beautiful black woman as well. When I was called the wrong name, she looked at me like, "So they think we're equal just because we're black."

After the meeting, I had a conversation with the other black woman. I told her how I felt about the meeting. She said that she felt the same way because we were black women. They would not have liked it if we called them not by their names. It's very disrespectful to not call someone by their name but expect that we are all the same. We all deserve respect, no matter who we are. If you don't know my name, ask me my name in the meeting. Don't just assume it's my name.

I DO NOT FEEL VALUED

Have you ever been in a position in your career where you felt you were not valued by the place you worked? Let's discuss a few red flags that I've seen throughout my career where I shouldn't be wasting my time and need to be moving on to another place where I might be appreciated as a human being.

I have been in positions in my career where I didn't feel valued by the place I worked. I should have put my resume in and started searching for a company that valued me as an individual with talent, not just as a diversity tag to say they had diversity.

Yes, I'm going to speak about not feeling confident in myself. I used to be a super nerd. I'm still a super nerd with confidence and self-awareness now that I have found the brand new me.

Working in your industry can make you unappealing in terms of your confidence due to the stress of dealing with work-related drama.

There are times when I wish I could just put on a hoodie and go to work and feel invisible. I did not want to go to work because I did not feel valued enough to do so. At times I only motivated myself to go to work because I cared about people who needed me. They didn't know that I cared, but I did. I didn't feel valued when I worked there. We all aspire to be treated equally and given equal opportunities and chances, but that's not what happens when you're in the minority in a corporate setting.

We often see these red flags and ignore them because we feel in our hearts and souls that things are going to get better, but they don't. As I started focusing on my career and figuring out this corporate life, it was a struggle for me. Some of the things that I experienced were being at the company for 12 months or less and then being told that you don't qualify for a raise/promotion. But you see other people who have been at the company less than 12 months getting promotions and advancing in their careers. This is a warning sign for the company to let you know that they are just here for the check at this time.

I've been in the same position for almost 3 years, and I haven't had a raise or promotion, but they thought that when I was sick of it, they could just give me a little raise and I'd stick around. I've seen a lot of people on the team, regardless of their talent, skillset, or even if they've worked at the company for a while, advance in their careers. The cost of living increases every year, and as I mentioned before, I am an independent woman who pays her own bills and does not have a husband to help me at all.

Being recognized by your employer will boost your self-esteem and give you an incentive to keep doing your best work and work hard.

I've worked at a couple of companies where I didn't feel valued and my culture wasn't represented. Because of this, having a lot of people you don't identify with can be tough. Also, most of the people in my generation are married or have kids.

I remember being on an uncomfortable Zoom call and I had nothing in common with anyone on the call. They were all first time parents, married or engaged. I was struggling to find a place to belong because I'm already feeling like an outsider in terms of culture and experiences. As a woman, I want to be a wife and a mother. One of the first things I noticed was that my culture had different perspectives on these topics.

Let along with this most of my peers at the moment are fresh out of college getting their first time experience with being in a corporate environment. It made me feel sad on the inside because I just did not feel this was a place I should have given much time to because I did not feel valued by this work culture. Now, as a result, I try to check out the culture online every once in a while to see what's going on. If I'm not seeing a ton of diversity, I don't think it's worth my time. You want to feel that you have something in common with someone.

I AM CHANGING

Yes, you heard it right, "I am changing". Every day that I'm opening my eyes to something new, I know it's another day that's giving me the chance to make a difference or find something new. Every day we should be open to learning something new or accepting more of who we've become. Some of our learning experiences are life lessons. It's good to be changed, and it's a good thing to hope for the best. I've come a long way since I was a young, impressionable girl. I've become a successful career woman.

All my work experiences have changed my life in one way or another. If you are setting your own standards like most selfish people do in the corporate world, that is not who you are. And we all need to learn how to set up a good working culture for any culture that comes into a new organization.

How can you listen effectively so that your voice is heard and not ignored because people have labeled you and are not mature enough to understand you and your work ethic?

When I think about my past and where I am in my career, I think about how I've changed as a person over the years. As I look back at my past, I'm thankful that I'm still that voice in the wilderness for other women out there who want to work in IT. I talk to other women sometimes, and we all go through the same struggles of feeling like we don't belong in a company that's so resistant to change.

As I reflect on those who have paved that way for us to do this. I am grateful that I am paving the way for other women as well. I have not had an easy career path with some of the struggles that I have come across but guess what it made me a better person and I have learned from it. Without the experiences that I have had I would not have been so inspired to write this book.

GIRL ON FIRE

*This is the final chapter of the book
and yes we are going to talk about
victories and accomplishments
throughout my career.*

I have arrived in the workplace and yes I have a flourishing career after everything I have been through. Celebrating yourself is a big accomplishment. Yes, everything is coming to me and my career is flourishing because I did not give up on myself. There's an old saying that says, "Pressure makes a diamond." I've been under a lot of pressure and I've turned into a diamond.

I have acquired many skills and gained a great wealth of knowledge from working every day in the Information Technology industry. From the beginning of my career in college to the beginning of a career where I didn't have much confidence in myself due to the challenges I faced.

"This Girl Is On Fire" by Alicia Keys. This song is one of my favorites. I bought this CD the day I bought my new car. I put this CD in my car, turned up the AC, and I just relished in the feeling that I was doing it all on my own. I know this is a little off topic but if I do hear this song in the story I am going to sing it. This album helped me stay inspired on making my dreams come true.

In this section, I'm going to discuss how this album has helped me become a more confident person, and hopefully, one day, Alicia Keys will get a copy of my book. Listening to "Brand New Me", this song describes how empowered I feel as a woman in Information Technology and being able to embrace myself and the path I choose. It wasn't easy, but it helped me become a better person.

I've crawled out of a cocoon to be this amazing woman and to keep on going. I've been lied to, cheated on, abused, mistreated, used, scorned, talked about like a sore as a bone, up, down, nearly to the ground. And guess what I became? As a woman, I knew we needed to make our voices heard, not just sit back and do nothing.

I will continue to shatter more glass ceilings and show the world that women are capable of anything they put their minds to and want to do. We all have the power to be that positive energy in the workplace.

There is only one life to live, and yes we must learn something new every day. Every day is a new adventure and how we embrace it. Every day I do my best to reach out to others with my big, big heart. At the end of the day, I hope I have shown some love to others and blessed them with my gifts and abilities. I hope I have left a legacy of being resilient in all that I do.

Listen to your heart. Think about your choices that you will make to prove this world wrong. This girl is on fire and has her eyes on the prize and on top of the world.

Maybe talk about being a wife and the new experiences of change to provide for my family and have a work life balance. I know I've always dreamed of being a mom, and I hope one day I can share my experiences of going through that life change and then transitioning into a body change and then giving birth and meeting that person.

I'm still proud of myself for taking the time to put pen to paper and write this heart-wrenching book. How I felt as a woman working in my field. How I hope the world will become more accepting of us as women in this field. The women who fought for women's rights in the past fought for the right to be who we want to be and to be who we aspire to be. I'm thankful for those women who fought for us.

FIN

*Thank you so much for buying my book
and for taking the time to encourage me.*

Writing this book was therapeutic for me because I had the opportunity to share all my experiences, struggles, unfairness, highs and lows.Now that I have finally let it all go, I feel free to share it. I want to help Women speak up in their work environment and be heard.Yes, I believe change is coming, slowly but surely.I will continue being who I am. If you don't like it, that's okay too. I am not going anywhere. And yes, I want to see more women pursuing careers in Information Technology, no matter what color they are. We can do this and I believe we have the courage to do this. I'm here to help inspire others who will become better in their lives. Some people aren't ready for this impact, but it's inevitable.

Don't let anyone downball you or devalue you by not listening.

Don't let anyone walk all over you or make you feel like you don't matter by not hearing you out. We're all different and we all have our own unique personalities, but in the end, we're gonna get it done.

I hope this book has been a great source of inspiration and I hope my story has helped you to see that you are not alone in some of these struggles.

Change in the workplace is always on the rise for the betterment of the world.